40 CCs of Inspiration
Inspirational Injections with Bradford Speaks

BRADFORD SPEAKS

Edited by: Candace Thoth & Ana M. Marcos

Photos Courtesy of: Candace Thoth - Founder, Return to Aloha

Aurora Rosselli - Eclisse Creazioni Art & Photography

Cover Designed by: Guillermo Reyes

40 CCs of Inspiration - Inspirational Injections with Bradford Speaks

Copyright © 2016 Bradford Speaks Life Publishing

All rights reserved. No part of this publication may be reproduced or transmitted in any form or by any means, without permission in writing from the author.

ISBN: 0692728007
ISBN-13: 978-0692728000

DEDICATION

This publication and the inspiration contained within are dedicated to my children – Jahna, Ty, Christyn, Blaise, Jackson and Claire - my biggest inspirations for all I do. Thank you Sabrina and Dana, for co-creating with me, enabling the vortex through which these beautiful Souls would port through to us. Thank you for the love in them that is manifested through our unions. Your love made me better.

The grandest of gratitude radiates from my being to the Infinite Creator; for the Divine Spark existent in us all, that inspired my Spirit and my hands to write. To my mother, Doris, who has always believed in my greatness – look, I did it Ma! ☺ To my siblings - Joe, Vicki, Daryl, and Judy; the balance of my family and friends, near, dear, and far; and to the many other co-creators who have made my life so exceedingly rich!

A very special thank you also goes out to Ana, my amazing partner, lover, supporter, reflection, teacher, friend, and fan; for understanding the artist that is me, and giving me the time and space needed to be solely focused on completing this and other labours of Love.

All my Love,

Bradford/Dad

Now…Let's get lifted – inspired – enlightened – Injected!

CONTENTS

	Acknowledgments	vii
1	Maintaining Life's Perfect Balance	Pg 9
2	Failure is Found in Giving Up	Pg 11
3	Your Life's Legacy	Pg 13
4	Ability, Motivation, Attitude	Pg 15
5	How Far is Too Far?	Pg 17
6	F.L.Y.	Pg 19
7	Go Where You Are Appreciated	Pg 21
8	The Meaning of Life	Pg 23
9	On Kindness	Pg 25
10	Goals are Nice, but Belief is the Driver	Pg 27
11	Would You Like to Meet You?	Pg 29
12	Only You Can Judge You	Pg 31
13	What Lies Within Matters Most	Pg 33
14	Take Care of You - for Me	Pg 35
15	The Love Rush	Pg 37
16	Be the BEST to You	Pg 39
17	There is Only NOW	Pg 41
18	Know Thyself	Pg 43
19	Change is Imminent	Pg 45
20	DNA of a Hero	Pg 47

21	Nothing is Impossible - NO Thing	Pg 49
22	Mine the Moments	Pg 51
23	Losing and Finding Yourself	Pg 53
24	Pray or Worry	Pg 55
25	Zen Master	Pg 57
26	A Strength Unknown	Pg 59
27	Visualize It . Feel It . Believe It	Pg 61
28	Rise	Pg 63
29	Life is A Game – Play it Well	Pg 65
30	No More Hiding	Pg 67
31	The Blame Game	Pg 69
32	This is the Way	Pg 71
33	Your Viewing Apparatus	Pg 73
34	The Greatness of Gratitude	Pg 75
35	Seek the Mystery	Pg 77
36	Conquering the Mountain that is You	Pg 79
37	Leave the Flower Be	Pg 81
38	The Beauty of Dying	Pg 83
39	You are Powerful	Pg 85
40	Being Right is Our Greatest Wrong	Pg 87
2X	Only Light Can Drive Out Darkness	Pg 89
	Mis Amores	Pg 90
	About the Author	Pg 91

ACKNOWLEDGMENTS

Since the inception of Life Architecture, Relationship Coaching & Speaking Firm, Bradford Speaks Life Management, *Inspirational Injections with Bradford Speaks*™ have been an integral part of the culture. With so much to share, I sought to build an audience of individuals who desire to raise their vibration and level of living by way of self-discovery and a deepened learning.

Inspirational Injections with Bradford Speaks™ started out with an intimate group of friends and family, then quickly expanded to touch hundreds of subscribers within the first year. The idea behind the concept was to provide quick, positive, and powerful life and thought-transforming messages that were also concise and easy to read. This would enable subscribers to get a brief 'dose' of inspiration and then move along with a happy and productive day in sight. As time went on, I began to incorporate video and audio accompaniments to the Injections. Some of the language here may seem a bit lofty, but we cannot reach for what we cannot at least first conceive with our imaginations. My intent is to stretch that very part of you through my gift of Word-smithing.

In this compilation, I have pulled together a powerful array of 40 *Inspirational Injections* I have shared with my audience over the last few years. Each of them begins with a quote or idea – some by folks you have heard of, some by unknown sources, and a few others penned by none other than yours truly. They are all loaded with the power to transform your thinking, broaden your perspectives, enhance your outlook, and deepen your interpretation of life as it moves through you. I would like you to allow the energy and intention that infuse my words, to spark within you a rapid shift towards the realization of your life's vision. May these words give you Life.

"Life is a balance of holding on and letting go." - Unknown

1 CC   MAINTAINING LIFE'S PERFECT BALANCE

The words in this quote are few, yet poignant. One of the primary things that keeps so many of us in bondage - and our lives in perpetual imbalance - is our unwillingness to let go of things that no longer serve us. Constantly and unapologetically evaluate and purge things that unnecessarily fill your life. Do this to determine what is excessive, and could potentially impede evolutionary growth. This also applies to relationships, whether romantic or platonic. Re-evaluate them regularly to verify that the return on your emotional investment is worthy of your continued deposits. Are your relationships yielding the value you initially hoped to receive from them, or are you simply remaining in them out of comfort, complacency, or perhaps a co-dependency that you may not yet be aware of?

Be bold and courageous enough to trim, prune, and cleanse the contents of your life - if, when, and where it is needed. Seek Infinite Wisdom to rid yourself of those things that fail to emanate what you want and need in order to propel you forward in the trajectory of your Life's Purpose. Scaling back or dissolving a relationship or two does not mean that love is no longer present; it only means that you have come to a place of knowing and loving yourself well enough to do what needs to be done to restore and maintain a healthy balance in your life.

Although all relationships and experiences have significant value in our lives, only you can judge whether something or someone is holding you back or helping you to grow. Only you can determine whether to keep holding on or to let it go.

"Our greatest weakness lies in the giving up. The most certain way to succeed is to always try just one more time." - Thomas Edison

2 CC   FAILURE IS FOUND IN GIVING UP

It isn't our fear of failure so much - as it is our fear of achieving greatness - that often causes us to quit prematurely. Far too often, just as we make the decision to give up, we later find that we were on the brink of a breakthrough had we just hung in there a little while longer. Funny how that works, isn't it? Giving up causes us to lose a tremendous amount of momentum – a force that can be very difficult, yet not impossible, to regain once we have turned away from the path we had previously set into motion. We shiver at the thought of having the lives, successes, and destinies of others in our hands. We quit because we aren't willing to make the sacrifices, and the (necessary) errors, to achieve our wildest dreams. Yes, charging forward in the face of your fears could mean rubbing up against extreme challenge, pain, difficulty, and perhaps even failure! Oh my! But, when you choose to quit, you are the one who has to carry the guilt of wondering "What if". So why not charge forward in the confidence of knowing you gave it your all? That is a guilt worth carrying, should you insist on carrying any guilt at all. I suggest not.

Put fear in its place once and for all. Care not what others may think. Move forth in the conviction that first awakened your heart to the dream living within you. Fear is an illusion, a mental construct of your very own creation. Do you like what you have made? If not, change it. Never fear giving it ONE MORE SHOT, for within every perceived failure lay the opportunity to put previous learnings to more intelligent future use.

Come on and say it with me. Allow the following phrase to resonate throughout your entire Being. Ready, set...go!

I WILL NEVER-EVER-QUIT!

"My life is my message."
– Mahatma Gandhi

3 CC   YOUR LIFE'S LEGACY

If you are honest, you would like to leave behind a legacy of some kind for yourself. On some level you think to yourself, *what is it that I want to be remembered for after I am no longer here in this physical form?* You want to be identified by your successors with something of great importance. You may aspire to be remembered for your body of work as an entertainer; a brave human rights activist; a world explorer and archeologist; a financial guru; an historian or educator; a writer; a businesswoman; a scientist or an astronaut; or maybe the best parent ever! Perhaps you want to be remembered as an incredibly gifted athlete who bedazzled millions with the skill and passion with which you played the game. Very few of us are happy with just being. We all want to be - ya know - great. Great at something! This all makes perfect sense; these desires define the nature of the Human Spirit.

The symphony of your legacy is being composed as you read this; your life's message is being written moment-to-moment. So, what is it that you are scribing? For most of us - as we grow older, more mature and wiser - we develop a deeper concern for what we are able to give and leave behind, and how it can positively impact and/or serve others. The words of mother begin to ring truer than ever before -"you can't take any of this with you when you go, so you'd better enjoy it while you are here!" As life moves forward, we become more enamored with what we will be remembered for in death, which culminates from what we do in life. The intangible fruits of our labor begin to take center stage in our future visioning.

If I may make a suggestion – choose now to make your legacy one that is enveloped in love, kindness, and compassion for others. These are the traits that are to be coveted and adored, even now.

So, what do you want to be remembered of you after The Game is over? Think about it, and then get busy writing *your* life's message!

"Ability is what you are capable of doing. Motivation determines what you will do. Attitude determines how well you will do it." – Unknown

4 CC   ABILITY . MOTIVATION . ATTITUDE

Abilities are the natural gift(s) we all possess to do something great - great being a highly subjective but relative term, of course. Just because you have not yet recognized what your natural abilities are, does not mean they are not present. It only means that you have yet to discover them. Even if you don't believe you have any special ability - any ability at all is special, and sufficient for doing something great.

What motivates you, though? In other words, what gets your engine revved up, and moving at a fast, deliberate and calculated pace? Our feelings or emotions about a thing - which are largely driven by our imagination - are what motivate (or motor) us to spring into action. Try this: Close your eyes for a moment. Go on, you can trust me. Now, imagine what it will feel like when you are living your decided Purpose; when you know beyond a shadow of a doubt that you are exactly where you are supposed to be. Who's there with you? What sounds do you hear? What are you saying to yourself? Ok, open your eyes. Did you feel that? That is the volcanic stillness of motivation, my friend; you can tap into that instantly - anytime, anywhere. There is a rarely understood peace and calm that follows this personal truth or knowing you are where your convictions are leading you; this peace and calm are yours for the taking.

Attitude is more potent than ability and motivation combined. Not just any attitude - but the right attitude. Attitude moves the depth of belief; it determines how well you will perform when utilizing your abilities. Attitude is an emotional and mental state that you can have right now, by simply choosing it. The right attitude wakes you up in the morning, excited about life. The right attitude determines how you will approach adversity. The right attitude can catapult anything you are doing, into utter greatness. In other words, Attitude - mixed with a heap of Motivation, and a dollop of Ability - is an indisputable recipe for success!

"Only those who risk going too far can possibly find out how far one can go." - T.S. Elliot

5 CC   HOW FAR IS TOO FAR

What is risk? This is a rhetorical question, as most of us already have some idea of its answer. But do respond to it internally, and see what you come up with. A bigger question regarding risk, however, would be:

What is risk in a sea of unlimited potentiality? The answer: Nothing.

Now this is a much broader question, and one that demands investigation. In either case, risk can mean something different to each of us, based upon how we view the world around us. Embedded deep within the very fabric of our Multi-verse is the potential for anything to happen, and the realization of such can open up a whole new world in which risk becomes irrelevant. Coming into a knowing that you *cannot* fail is extremely empowering. The way you define failure changes upon the recognition of the vast combination of possibilities that available to you – infinite possibilities. You can't go too far, because too far is not possible – not within a sea of potentiality that knows no bounds.

Two things I can attest to:

1) No one has ever achieved greatness without taking risks.

2) Fear is the primary culprit behind your reluctance to reach toward new and uncomfortable heights.

Ask yourself: What would I do if I knew I could not fail? What risks would I be willing to take?

Whatever your answers, it is high time for getting down to the business of doing it; moving forward in the confidence that you CANNOT FAIL. And you won't. Will you. Of course not.

"F.L.Y. – First. Love. Yourself – Others will come next." – Bradford Speaks

6 CC   F.L.Y.

In this New Age of Enlightenment that is upon us, again, we have yet another chance to create a new and more desirable world in which to live. There is much chatter today around the importance of self-love, much more than in our most recent past, it seems. Not so much from a place of selfishness and neglect towards others, persay, but in a way that suggests an emerging realization of the Oneness that intrinsically connects us all. We are certainly playing in the correct sandbox when concepts such as self-love are top of mind. Though a slow and gradual process, large swaths of humanity seem to be on the verge of re-discovering the secrets to living fully, happily, and fearlessly. And with the tools now readily available to us, states of mind and emotion can be attained at accelerated rates.

The root emotions of fear and Love directly affect our actions; their continuous collisions combust to create the contrast which forms the life-dream we experience. If we will allow our actions to be driven primarily by the latter of these two emotions - Love - our world will become greater as a result. It is often said that we cannot truly Love another until we first Love ourselves. It is cliché, but it is very true. You must first gain an inner-standing of what Love really is. How? By becoming a student of Love, just as you do with any other subject matter you wish to master. To become a student of Love means to become a student of the Self, because at your very core, YOU are Love. So in learning who YOU are, you will subsequently discover what Love is. The pursuit of this mastery must become a consuming passion. Love must become your culture - your normal - your religion.

We tend to place most of our attention on learning how to Love others, and how to make them happy. We exert enormous amounts of energy into finding others to give our Love to, as opposed to giving it to ourselves. Once you learn to Love you, attracting Love from others becomes an effortless task. Loving you begins with knowing and accepting the whole complexity of who you are. Learning to Love yourself is truly the greatest Love of all.

"Don't stay where you are tolerated; go where you are celebrated." - Unknown

7 CC   GO WHERE YOU ARE APPRECIATED

So many of us remain in situations and relationships - jobs/careers, living arrangements, romances, friendships, etcetera - that fail to celebrate who we are. We sit glued in these situations even though the others involved couldn't care less about who we really are, or the value we add to their lives. We know that in these situations we are only being tolerated, yet we have conditioned ourselves to be okay with it. Never raising your hand to say, "hey, I deserve so much more, and to be treated better." You may not believe that you do, which is why you don't express a demand for it. We are uncomfortable and miserable with where we currently are in life, but out of fear of encountering some discomfort, we remain in the same place until we make ourselves literally sick – physically sick and sick of ourselves.

Awareness is your saviour! **Awareness** empowers you, and makes you responsible for making the necessary changes for moving into a celebratory situation - one that salutes every intricate detail of who you are. You are more than worthy of being celebrated, don't you agree??

Declare **TODAY** the day you break free of these chains.
There is no better time than **NOW**!

From within the womb of awareness, a sincere desire to create change is birthed. Now through meditation, begin visualizing, attracting, and surrounding yourself with the love and appreciation you know you deserve. Allow those who want to love and celebrate you, to love and celebrate you. Let them exalt and praise you; to cradle you in pure adoration. Gravitate toward those whose primary interests lay in seeing you happy, growing, and thriving! Be discriminate of whom and what you lend this exclusive access into your life. You are worthy.

"What is the meaning of life? Whatever you want it to be." – James Frey

8 CC   THE MEANING OF LIFE

As human beings, it is not uncommon to ponder the meaning of life during the course of our lifetimes. It is a **BIG IDEA** that only the individual can ascribe any substantial meaning to. Sometimes we will deliberate it internally, within the private caverns of our minds. Other times we may be a bit more vocal in our inquisition. This contemplative process is both healthy and natural. It is this single wondering – **Who Am I?** – that sparks all human expansion. We *want* to know more about our origins - how we arrived on this planet, who or what placed us here, and are they still watching or involved on any level? Most importantly, we want to know *why* we are here; what is our purpose for existing? What should we be *doing* during our limited time here, which is daily coming to an end? What happens when it is all over? Is it ever really over, or does it all simply end just to begin again?

Well, there is certainly Meaning, as well as Purpose to life. The Meaning of life is not synonymous with its Purpose; however, they are very closely related. Many use the terms interchangeably in their search to make sense of the mystery of life, but make no mistake, they are different. The **Meaning of Life** is simply this: to exist; to Be - to bathe in experience. That is all. There are no expectations of you to Be or to experience life in any particular way, as such expectation would be a violation of the birthright of Free Will given you by your Creator. The rest of life's Meaning fulfills itself through you. To see it any other way only limits the experience.

In contrast, **Life's Purpose** is individualized, and varies based on the individual's desire for a particular set of experiences. This is why Life Purposes are so diverse. It would be best described as *Your* Life's Purpose. Purpose is driven by dominant desires - meaning that whatever desires, thoughts, and dreams permeate and burn deepest within the Soul - direct Life's Purpose. Your task is to identify these dominant desires, match them with your natural gifts and talents, and then mold it all into something really marvelous, exquisite, and unique.

"Be kind to unkind people; they are the ones who need it most." – Unknown

9 CC   ON KINDNESS

Kill 'em with kindness – Many of us have no doubt heard this phrase before when being encouraged to choose kindness in the face of someone else's disgrace. This can be a difficult task because the emotions that drive our actions often signal for a conditioned and seemingly automated response to fight back, to protect and defend who we perceive ourselves to be. We respond as if it is a personal attack, and perhaps sometimes it is. But is it real? And don't we always have a choice in how we respond? Most often, a great desire to reciprocate the unkindness being projected toward us rises up on the inside. When this happens, mentally dissociate yourself from the situation. In your mind's eye, envision yourself now standing outside of your body, observing the poison being spewed from that person towards you. Now, picture the possibilities of what pain they might have experienced as a child, an adolescent, or an adult. Picture the possible misery surrounding their life, and their inner struggle to find true joy in life. This is Empathy and Compassion in action.

Kindness has the capacity to change our world, but it must manifest itself through you. Kindness breeds compassion. Compassion enables you to see others through a different lens - a lens that helps you to see correlations between your life's journey and that of others'. Compassion enables us to imagine ourselves in their shoes.

Those who spread such misery to others are often totally unaware as to why. It is because they are in pain, and this poison they carry within originates from a severe lack of happiness and contentment within their own lives. Identify this pain within them; accept it for what it is, then refrain from reacting negatively to it. Remember that just like the poison, kindness can also be infectious. Kindness is the antidote to a mean spirit. YOU may be the only example of authentic kindness someone ever sees, so make sure you are a damned good one! **Go**. Be kind to someone today.

"Goals are the fuel in the furnace of achievement." – Unknown

10 CC   GOALS ARE NICE, BUT BELIEF IS THE DRIVER

Belief drives our course of action in life. When we possess strong belief about a thing, we are more willing to take risks - risks that support that belief. With belief, no risk is perceived by the mind; belief places us in complete trust of our thoughts and decisions. Belief pushes us down a particular path, and the stronger belief grows, our momentum down that path grows synchronously. When we believe in our ability to successfully perform a task (or not), we are more likely to attempt it (or not).

Goals are just concepts until they are infused with belief, which allows them to penetrate the physical world. Belief is necessary to provide the foundation and supporting cast for goals. It is not a lack of goal setting that is the problem, but a lack of belief that those goals can actually be attained. Therefore, by focusing on changing disempowering belief systems and implementing new and empowering ones, you can 'fan the flames' of the goals you have set.

So, what is a belief? A belief is repetitive thought that lingers in the unconscious mind, erecting the pillars that fashion our reality. Beliefs are a feeling of great conviction that something is true. They are ideas, subtly fed into the conscious mind, often forming boundaries that tend to enclose and limit or expand us. Expanding your belief in what you can achieve, introduces a world of unlimited possibilities. When this constant stream of focused thought/belief is positive, and is then attached to a goal, this becomes the fuel that propels us. For instance, money would have absolutely no power at all if we did not believe it did. If we believe that having money is the key to achieving a goal we have set, then the absence of money will yield the opposite effect. The belief that money is a necessity is what drives us to obtain it so that we can fuel the furnace of our visions. If you were to believe that a litter of kittens would provide you with the same ability to achieve your goals, the results would be very much the same. If you could will yourself to believe it, you have the power to move mountains. So what do you want to believe about yourself? **DECIDE.**

"Be the type of person you want to meet."
– Unknown

11 CC   WOULD YOU LIKE TO MEET YOU?

There really is no point in complaining about the kind of people we attract into our lives, though it is a complaint we all hear rather frequently. Many will say to themselves:

> **Why can't I find someone to love me the way I love him or her?**
> **Why do I continually attract negative people into my life?**
> **Why do people seem to always take advantage of and misuse me?**

Sound familiar? Perhaps you have asked yourself these questions. They are valid inquiries, and should not go ignored. Actually, they should send bright, orange flares hurling through your soul, signaling to you - **here** is where work needs to be done! This kind of self-interrogation can wreak havoc on your relationships - both with others and with ourselves - especially when not answered in a healthy and constructive way.

Be careful not to exert so much energy into the type of people you are attracting. Instead, focus your attention on the type of person you are, and who you desire to be. It is understandable to want to attract good people into your experience; people who make you feel good, and will enrich the wholistic quality of your life. When you work daily to sculpt the best YOU, you will find that the reflection of that perfection in YOU will organically find its way to you.

Remember: One aspect of life's journey is YOU looking back at yourself through the mirrors of your relationships, and you are in relationship with every-single-thing. Do you like the person you see? If not, utilize your relationships as one tool to bring into greater focus the person you most want to be. When all is said and done, you should be able to look at anyone and anything, and see yourself. And oh my, lookie, lookie! Aren't you just beautiful!

> **YOU are the beauty in this world**

"You alone are the judge of your worth, and your goal is to discover infinite wealth in yourself, no matter what anyone else thinks." – Deepak Chopra

12 CC   ONLY YOU CAN JUDGE YOU

The joy of finally reaching a point in life where you know the weight of your worth - and that it is truly immeasurable – is such a wonderful place to arrive. Realizing that you, and only you, are the one qualified to judge this colossal worth. Many of us rarely get here; we allow 'life' to get in the way of discovering at a deep level who and what we really are.

Coming to this profound realization is where life begins to open up like the petals of a flowering lotus. Most of us derive our worth from a place of object referral - through the comparison of objects outside of ourselves. Examples are: money, success, material possessions, wealth, social or economic status, employment or relationship status, the car we drive, the exotic trips and vacations we are able to take, the home we live in, the gadgets we possess, even down to the prestige of the neighborhood we reside in. This also works conversely with those who have little; when a person does not possess much, they must refer to a different place to acquire their own sense of self-worth. Their worth may come from the pride of cultural traditions, close-knit family ties, and cherished friendships - those things that are a bit more intangible for them.

Our personalities, egos, and socioeconomic statuses are not who we are, but the deep connection and relationships we might have with them can certainly cause us to believe so. To truly know your worth, you must realize - and digest as truth – that you may not be who you have always believed you were. You must reveal unto your Self that you are much more than your brain could ever comprehend. You must recognize that you are a part of something so, so grand. Base your worth on this knowledge and embark upon a life-long journey of discovery. Judge your Self by this premise. Once you discover your true worth, thoughts of 'I can't' will wither away. You will know that there is no place to arrive to by any particular point in time; that there are no deadlines, and no such thing as failure. You couldn't fail even if you tried. You are loved beyond your wildest fantasies, and worth more than you may ever fully grasp. Only you can judge you – judge righteously.

"What lies behind us and what lies before us, are tiny matters compared to what lies within us."
– Oliver Wendell Holmes

13 CC WHAT LIES WITHIN MATTERS MOST

It's easy to know what lies behind us because we have already experienced it; we can recall and relive it again at will. We can vividly see the people, jobs, careers, relationships passed, life-changing events, and choices that lay in our wake. We can draw a number of conclusions and lessons from these as well. The past is limited by time. We cannot turn back the clock and change what has already transpired; we can only change how we view and feel about it, and such can be highly transformative. It is relatively easy to know what lies before us, because much of it we plan out in our minds before it ever occurs. Life's circumstances have a funny way of creeping in and altering our plans, but we can – to a large degree - know what our day-to-day is going to look like. What lies before us is also limited, and in no way compares to what lies within us.

What lies inside us - oh boy! This is the part that is highly unknown – it is the *X Factor*, which makes it most curious. What lies within us is pure, unlimited potentiality. Most humans live an entire lifetime not having scratched the surface of their true potential. Even when we think we have reached our limits, life cries out, "No, keep going; there is more there to be had!" We learn some minor aspects of what lies inside us when we are faced with challenging life situations. We take those moments far too lightly; we fail to bookmark those events so that we may draw strength from their recall during what seems to be inevitable future times of struggle and suffering. The recollection of these experiences is an invaluable tool for transformation, and should be leaned upon to bolster confidence in the etherically astonishing stuff we are made of.

The fact remains - the potential for greatness and the immense resolve hidden within, can only be discovered by experiences requiring us to dig deep into the reservoirs of the Soul, testing our supposed limits. In doing so, we realize that limitations are illusions. Each time we are tried - if we remain aware - we can clearly see that there is no end to what we can achieve. **From the inside out, You are amazing; live and walk in your amazing-ness**.

"The greatest gift you can give to somebody is your own personal development. I used to say, 'if you will take care of me, I will take care of you.' Now I say, 'I will take care of me for you, if you will take care of you for Me'." – Jim Rohn

14 CC   TAKE CARE OF YOU – FOR ME

Wow! What a powerful and innovative approach towards achieving self-love; certainly a break from the traditional way in which we have typically come to define personal development. Personal development is such a key and vital element in finding happiness and creating authentic and abundant joy in our lives. When we fail to develop ourselves, we fail everything and everyone who shares our lives with us.

Historically, we have seen personal development as a work being done on the individual, and for the benefit of the individual only; the phrase 'personal development' implies this very notion. But another concept is now coming into view – one that acknowledges the connectivity of personal development to the development of an individual's entire aural microcosm; meaning everything that is connected to them in both the physical and non-physical realms. The caveat to the idea of personal development that mustn't go unnoticed is the fact that **we don't develop ourselves only for ourselves; we do it so that everything and everyone around us benefits as well**. And we are no good for anyone else until we are first good for ourselves. When we are at our very best, everything near and around us thrives.

There is no particular pace at which you are required to move along your path of personal development. Actually, movement isn't a requirement at all. But, it is a necessity if one aspires to exceed his/her own expectations. Stagnancy (or the lack of energy in motion) causes complacency, and complacency breeds discontent. Energy likes to move, so let it – and let it do so in a positive direction. Continuously maneuver towards uncovering the greatest parts of yourself, knowing that this will reveal the greatness of everything that encircles you.

"Don't rush into any kind of relationship. Work on yourself, feel yourself, experience yourself. Do this first, and you will soon attract that special loving other." - *Russ von Hoelscher*

15 CC — LOVE RUSH

Many of us have rushed into relationships – be it business and/or personal. Our emotions have such power to cause us to move quickly and impulsively. This isn't all bad. There are no mistakes; there is only experience and lessons coming in various forms. These moments of anxiety present grand opportunities to advance the learning that is facilitated by the body.

Romantic relationships seem to embody the most pressure, so we will focus on those. Most of the burden we feel - to find that *one true love* in life - is self-induced. We allow society to dictate where we should be by a certain point in life. This pressure is most notable in the lives of women. Her ability to attract a husband - in many societies - is a direct indication of her value and worth. This is grotesque, ludicrous, and grossly unfair. Not having 'found love' by the time we are supposed to, can create feelings of inadequacy and fear that something might be wrong with us. Failed relationships can also feed this fear and uncertainty of self.

In search of this love that we are so certain is awaiting us out there, we lose who we are. In fact, more often than not, we've never really known who we were to begin with; which makes the witch hunt to 'find love' even more daunting. What we are really searching for is ourselves. Socialization presents many inherent challenges with discovering who we are beyond what we have been taught. This eagerness to find love, as opposed to seeking out quality relationships that are bursting with prospects to bond with our other-selves, can leave us clutching a flashlight in broad daylight, searching for a love that is omni-present.

Every relationship is drawn into your vortex for the purpose of your evolution. Each encounter provides you with additional canvas space on which to stroke a new and improved version of yourself. The work of discovering You is never-ending, and the rush to find love outside can obstruct this most important discovery of all. There is really no need to rush, no matter your years. Slow your roll – Love is right there; yes, riiiiight there.

"Be very good to others, but be the BEST to yourself." – Bradford Speaks

16 CC   BE THE BEST TO YOU

You have got to be good to you, no matter what! I implore it! Many of you have a heart to serve, but chances are the design of modern society has led you to compete instead. Because of this, that part of you which desires to be of Service, is neglected and malnourished. Your desire to serve yourself is also malnourished, and this, my friend, is the greater issue. You cannot be truly good to others without being the very BEST to yourself. It is not possible to serve others at the highest level, while simultaneously short-changing yourself.

An intense energetic exchange takes place when you serve others with sincere intention of heart, mind and spirit. You are giving away tiny pieces of yourself, and those tiny pieces can quickly accumulate to form large chunks that must at some point be replenished. Lack of replenishment for long periods of time will mitigate the effects of your giving.

How do you make certain you are being the BEST to yourself?

Take regular time out for yourself. Do things *you* enjoy doing – things that bring *you* extreme joy. Read a book that arouses your Soul, whisking your mind away on journeys to distant places on the wheels of your imagination. Mental excursions are powerful - they enhance perspectives and expand worldviews. Travel to other countries, immersing yourself in foreign cultures; your social barometer will evolve. Treat yourself to a quiet dinner alone; go to the zoo; take a hike and commune with nature; spend a day at the beach; treat yourself to a massage; grill out with friends. These are just a few examples of ways in which you can be good to yourself, and in turn be a phenomenal lover of your other-selves (everyone else who is also a part of you, making up the whole of the planet). The quality time you give to yourself is far more valuable than any time you could give in Service To Others. Love yourself - care for yourself - be the BEST to yourself. **Always**.

"Un-ease, anxiety, tension, stress, worry- all forms of fear, are caused by too much future and not enough presence. Guilt, regret, resentment, grievances, sadness, and all forms of non-forgiveness are caused by too much past and not enough presence." - Eckhart Tolle

17 CC   THERE IS ONLY NOW

Life can bring on great feelings of un-ease, tension, stress, and worry. These feelings are caused by a lack of presence, and too much time spent in future thought. Life can also invite in feelings of guilt, regret, resentment, sadness, and the like, which are also caused by too much past and not enough presence. The truth of the matter is that life itself brings on none of this, as many of us so erroneously believe. It is the lack of presence in our lives that welcomes in these negative emotional states and mental strees, which often manifest in the body as sickness and dis-ease. It is **we** who are responsible for this deficiency of presence.

What does Mr. Tolle mean in his use of the term *presence*? Presence, by definition, has several meanings; but the one we will use to illustrate this particular narrative is mental existence in place. Mental existence in place simply means to exist - or to BE - *only* in the (mental) place you are in, in every moment in time; not a minute before or later. It means being right here (**only**), right now (**only**) – physically, mentally, and emotionally – focused solely on present moments (**only**), as each pixelated frame of life appears before you. Although time never stands still, you can create stillness in your life that will grace you with the power to remain in a space of complete happiness and healing for as long as you live. Allowing your thoughts and awareness to remain engulfed in past experiences or future possibilities, is not the path for creating a life filled with bliss and beauty. Only by remaining in the **NOW** - in This Present Moment - can we experience the beauty of life that is before us, and the positive emotions associated with living a life filled with presence.

So…where are you right now? Is that where you want to be?

If not, then come back to the **Present**. And with each and every move you make, *stay* there.

"To know another is wisdom, but to know thyself is enlightenment." – Unknown

18 CC   KNOW THYSELF

It is the true work of your life to master the Self. An ancient Egyptian proverb states: **Man, know thyself**. Were you aware that this is the task for those choosing to live life in their highest state of conscious Being? How close are you to mastering You? Have you yet begun? If not, I have some good news – if you are reading this, it isn't too late!

What does it mean to 'Master the Self'? Many of us feel that we know the people in our lives pretty well, but it is arguable just how well we actually know them. It is arguable because so often we are disappointed by the moves and decisions made by those we claim to know so well. I contend that we only know a person's tendencies, and are unable to fully predict their moves on any permanent basis. The unpredictability is one of the traits that makes homo-sapiens so unique among living species. Many of us know others in our lives better than we know ourselves, and that just isn't the way it should be. It is YOU who is supposed to be your own subject of mastery. This is *your* journey; one in which you will surely pick up occasional passengers to accompany you along the way. These relationships enable us to see compounded aspects of ourselves through the kaleidoscope they are able to provide us.

My intent is not to devalue the lives of those who fill your days with experiential joy, but to cause you to amplify the value you place upon your own journey toward the Mastery of your Self. This is not a selfish doctrine I am encouraging, but a Self doctrine. The journey to Self-mastery is one to be walked alone - without fear - and with a myriad of Soul mates cheering you on from within the shadows of the aisles.

All paths inherently intersect at a common point, segueing toward connecting you with your inner Buddha - the light inside of you, yearning to burn bright and hot. Happy Trails!

"There is nothing in life more certain than change." – Bradford Speaks

19 CC   CHANGE IS IMMINENT

The Universe at Large is filled with constant change. In fact, our very bodies are changing by the moment, as billions of cells die each second, and new ones take their place. Bologically you aren't the same person you were just hours ago…a few minutes more and you've changed again. This change is very gradual, and unending. Science has also proven that even though from our Earthly perspective the cosmos appear to be calm, quiet, and peaceful, it is violently chaotic, and teeming with the stuff of life! Meteors and asteroids are flying around our solar system, and throughout space at thousands of miles per hour, colliding with other space-occupying matter. Supernovae are occurring light years away from us; distant solar systems, once viewable, can no longer be seen – proving the constant expansion of our Multi-verse. *Continental drift* is happening daily, right underneath the soles of our feet.

Get used to change quickly – it is what all of life is comprised of. The sooner you can accept that change is both imminent and inevitable - and that it is the most certain thing that we can be certain of - the better equipped you become to maneuver through obstacles as they move towards you. They will come - those abrupt, life-altering events that rock the foundations of our lives; those events that force us to regroup entirely in order to manage turbulent and unexpected shifts. How we choose to react to change is a vital key to blissful living.

Obstacles occur in cycles, and they only remain for as long as we need them to - we can push them away whenever we are ready. Just like pushing away from the dinner table once we are satisfied. There's no use in fighting with it. Acquiescence to change makes life a lot more palatable. **Peace** rides gunshot with the embracement of change.

We can't always control the change that is happening outside of us, but we have total control of what happens inside — and truth is, it is all on the inside. Focus on that.

"A hero is an ordinary individual who finds extraordinary strength to persevere and endure in spite of overwhelming obstacles." - Christopher Reeve aka Superman

20 CC   DNA OF A HERO

Who is your hero? What does the word 'hero' mean to you? My list of heroes is long; there are a number of individuals whose strength and passion I have admired. Our definitions will, no doubt, vary. We all have those who have somehow touched and inspired our lives.

Personally, I define a hero as <u>one who is brave – who is willing to stand tall in the face of affliction, and particularly in defense of those who aren't yet strong enough to stand up for themselves</u>.

She is one who is not afraid to swim upstream against what is popular; she welcomes a challenge, and will not back down from what she believes is in the best interest of the greater good. A hero has character and poise.

An example of what a hero is to me: The firemen (and women), policemen (and women), EMS and building workers who were present during America's attack of the World Trade Center in New York City, on September 11, 2001. I have often asked myself, what would I have done if I were there on that day? When hero is in your DNA, you don't wake up on a particular day with a plan to go out and be a hero. An event happens, and you simply step up to the plate; your response is purely reactionary. These heroes rushed inside of burning, collapsing buildings, in an attempt to save the lives of complete strangers. They looked death square in the eyes, knowing the trip inside could be one-way, and possibly end up as their gravesite. ***That*** is what I consider to be heroic! Heroes - in a particular frame in time - conquer death. Those Americans were true heroes - perhaps the greatest of an entire decade.

You are extraordinary in every way imaginable! You have within you the DNA of a hero.

Who are your heroes? How do you define a hero? Whose hero are you?

"If a thing is humanly possible, consider it to be within your reach." – Marcus Arelius

21 CC   NOTHING IS IMPOSSIBLE – NO THING

Human potentiality has been questioned and challenged for millions of years throughout the course of our evolution. It is one of the primary reasons for the emergence of competitive sporting among the Ancient Greeks. With this constant pushing of the envelope, we have discovered so much about what humans are capable of – such as how to create fire for cooking food and keeping warm in cold temperatures. Pushing the limits of human potentiality sparked the skill of wood and stone works for the purposes of cutting, and over the course of time the craft of metallurgy would emerge from these.

The driving force of human curiosity have throughout antiquity led to deep explorations of space, its constellations, and our own solar system via the use of high-powered telescopes and rocket-fueled propulsion technologies. With all of these outstanding and daunting re-discoveries, one can see how easy it could be to lose sight of the vast possibilities that are within one's own reach. These great achievements are icons for pointing humanity forward; a beacon for aiding it to see just what is humanly possible. For each of us individually, they are to serve as benchmarks of the possibilities existent within us.

Without daring and brave men and women, whose curiosity to know more, be more, go further, ignore boundaries, and in many cases stretching toward what to many seemed to be impossible - we would not know that No Thing is impossible – if we can only believe. We would not know that limits are only 'slights of hand' being played on us by the mind. We would not know what it means to consider all things that can be conceived in thought, to be humanly possible - attainable even. Whatever you can dream up is entirely within your reach.

Dream bigger. Reach higher. Nothing is impossible!

"Mining the moment for something that feels good, something to appreciate, something to savor, something to take in, that's what your moments are about...

...they're not about justifying your existence. It is justified. You exist. It's not about proving your worthiness. It's done. You are worthy. It's not about achieving success. You never get it done. It's about 'How much can this moment deliver to me?' And some of you like them fast, some of you like them slow. No one's taking score. You get to choose. The only measurement is between your desire and your allowing. And your emotions tell you everything about that." - Abraham

22 CC   MINE THE MOMENTS

How are you spending your moments? Are you diligently mining them for those 'feel good' emotions? Throw out those duds, and set your intention to harvest only those moments that bring you extreme delight. Only hold onto the things you like. Toss the undesirable outcomes back into the Multi-verse's infinite ocean to be re-absorbed; perhaps someone else can make better use of them. Re-cast your rod, and reel in what you *do* want. Isn't this what life is, really? Gathered moments strung together upon an invisible thread, creating this construct we refer to as "time" - neatly divided into years, months, weeks, days, hours, minutes, and seconds. Forget about time; an incredible creative force such as you cannot be restricted by the ticking hands of a clock. Focus instead on living moment to moment, lending closer attention to the lucid details of life. Once you master the art of finding the happiness hidden within the moment – a gentle breeze; the fluttering wings of a hummingbird outside your window; a bumble bee pollinating a budding flower; or the laugh of a toddler – you won't have time to think about what miseries your mind attempts to conjure up from your past, or what it claims awaits you tomorrow.

So pull out your mining gear and hit the caves! Search out those golden moments that make life so succulent! If you find a nugget that isn't big enough, shiny enough, or isn't the shape you like, gift it away, and continue digging until you find exactly what you love. Keep your most joyous moments alive by sharing them - this will provide you with residual joy in the form of memories. Be patient - find contentment in the moments, and excitedly anticipate whatever lies ahead!

"It is in seeking the acceptance and approval of others that we so often lose ourselves."
– Bradford Speaks

23 CC   LOSING AND FINDING YOURSELF

Have you ever lived any part of your existence expending all of your mental, emotional and physical energy just to please another person? Have you participated in relationships where all that mattered to you was being able to meet their expectations of you? No matter how lofty you knew they were, you still desperately tried to meet them. Can you catch yourself, still today, remaining accountable to *their* standards, even though they have long departed from your life? You can still hear them criticizing the way you did a particular thing, or demeaning your line of thinking. Today you will crush the gavel they've held over your life.

These people – regardless of what suffering they brought your way – are some of the most important guides of your life. Your experience with them was never meant to imprison you, but to free you. As previously mentioned, every relationship has purpose, and it is simply to help you to see You better – a clearer and more refined version of You. They provide a compass for finding your way home whenever you're lost, drifiting inside The Dream. Though it may not feel like it at the time, each savoire faire has the very same intention of keeping you centered, but can only do so if you are paying close attention. As children we are conditioned into patterns of approval seeking – from parents, teachers, community or religious leaders, older siblings, even friends. For the most part they all had well-intentioned expectations of us. But seeking – and perhaps being unable to obtain these approvals from the most important people in our lives – can have significantly negative effects on the acceptance of ourselves, by ourselves. It can affect how we ultimately perceive our self-worth, becoming lost inside the matrix of our own life.

The great injustice is not the people placing this judgment upon us; the injustice is in our allowance of it. We should be held by no other standards, save for our own; and when we are living life in a high state of Consciousness, our standards are quite sufficient. **Develop your own standards, or else you are destined to be governed by someone else's.**

"Either pray or worry; don't do both."
– Curtis Jackson aka 50 Cent

24 CC   PRAY OR WORRY

These are the simple, yet profound words of rapper Curtis Jackson aka 50 Cent, stated in an Oprah Winfrey interview in 2012. **"Either pray or worry; don't do both**." You certainly can do both if you want, but what's the point? If you pray now, and then five minutes later you are still worrying about the thing you just prayed about, why even put forth the effort to pray in the first place? Some of the biggest 'prayer warriors' are also the biggest worrywarts. What an oxymoron! Even the longest, most fervent and sweat-filled prayer won't yield you the results you seek if you don't believe and have confidence in its eventual manifestation.

It is my position that if we truly believe, our prayers will be answered - there is no need to continue making the same requests over and over again. The Infinite Creator is only tuned into the speech of your heart; the words we speak do have power, yes, but they are ancillary to our thoughts. Law of Attraction is a close relative of prayer; some would even say they are born of the same womb - I would agree. All of the great Master Teachers who have come before us, believed their prayers were reaching 'heaven', and if the outcome they prayed for never came to fruition, they accepted it as part of the human experience. The number of times we pray has no bearing on how quickly, or even *if* that prayer will be answered.

When you truly believe that someone is going to perform a favor you have asked of them, how many times do you go back and submit the same request? Do you ask again and again, or do you remain patient, allowing them the time to get it done? Pray as often as you like, but the repetition isn't necessary — not when you believe all things good come your way. Accept that as long as you are in a body, 'suffering' comes with the gig. We can mitigate suffering by remembering that: **no matter how real an experience may feel, it is an illusion, created by you in The Game of Life that you have chosen to play**. The 'let go and let GOD' that so many speak about, works, but only if you actually **let go**. So pick one: Pray - or worry.

"When you try to stay on the surface of the water, you sink; but when you try to sink, you float." – Zen

25 CC   ZEN MASTER

If you are one who is able to swim, this quote makes you stop and think to yourself…*wait a minute, what?* Oh yeah, that's true! But whether you can swim or not, I am sure you will concur that staying on the surface of the water is the objective, and is also what we struggle to do in the sea of life. On the surface is where the warm sunshine finds the crown of our heads and comforts us; on the surface is where we find oxygen, and the peace of breath. We exert an extreme amount of effort to stay afloat, and often times we end up sinking as a result – simply because *trying* to stay afloat is counterproductive. The pressures and stresses of life can attack us from many angles, dragging us to and fro like a helpless leaf flailing in the wind. But is it really helpless? Or is it just going with the flow, taking it all in as it comes?

The balance we seek in life is delicate; there is an art involved in obtaining and maintaining it. We have to find life's natural 'ebb and flow'; the vibration, the sound that life emits. Some go to the extremes of ignoring the craziness as though it isn't there. This is resistance, and whatever we resist, only persists. Resistance in some cases is necessary, however, because it forges a persistence which is useful for experiencing something for the purpose of contrast. Contrast helps to clarify the areas in our life that need work. The goal is not to dwell in the resistance, but to recognize it, acknowledge it, and then float on through it.

Here are a few effective tools for treading life's currents:

1) **Be Patient** – with yourself; less trying and more Being.
2) **Acknowledge & Validate** - Let life know that you are aware of its presence.
3) **Meditate More** - Think less. Allow positivity to dominate your thoughts.
4) **Make Peace** – Control what you can; make peace with what you cannot.

Float On

"You never know how strong you are until being strong is your only choice."
– Bob Marley

26 CC   A STRENGTH UNKNOWN

You couldn't possibly know, could you, if every situation always turned out perfectly? How would you learn of your inner resolve when faced with life's inevitable adversities, if everything came to you so easily? How else, other than through so-called tribulation, would you know that leaning into the discomforts of the human experience is your biggest asset for learning that you are <u>always</u> going to come out fine on the other side? Upon what would you build such resolve if there were no objections to confront? Your strength must be built upon previous experience, which does none other than prepare you, proving to you that **you can**!

It is when we are faced with what we perceive as life's toughest contests, that we discover the unfathomable resilience we possess inside. Just like the Summer foliage changes from shades of green, to oranges and browns as Fall settles in, so do our lives reach points of unavoidable change and transformation. As the trees 'suffer' in order to make way for Spring's incoming beauty, it is our suffering that generates the beauty that is alive inside of us. This beauty cannot come forth without struggle, any more than a diamond can be forged without extreme heat, pressure, and fine craftsmanship. Struggles are what make the symmetry in life so radiant and memorable. Knowing that you have overcome one obstacle, increases your belief that you can – and will – overcome the next.

When your back is against the wall, and the only choice you are given is to be strong, you surprise yourself with what you can endure. There is no mountain you cannot conquer, no valley you cannot climb out of; there isn't a situation you cannot dig your way through. There is so much love and support surrounding you. If you would only dare look inward, you will find every single thing you need - a strength you always knew was present.

Be strong.

"Visualize this thing you want. See it. Feel it. Believe in it. Make your mental blueprint and begin." – Robert Collier

27 CC   VISUALIZE IT . FEEL IT . BELIEVE IT

Everything ever created began with an initial thought - yes, **EVERYTHING**! Even matter itself. Thought is pure, concentrated Energy, formed first from within the realm of Spirit, that when intensely focused, becomes a picture or mental photograph. This image then maps over to, and projects onto the mind's eye, and with reverberating, meditative thought, eventually creates what is called a vision. A **vision** - when showered with constant focus and attention - becomes clearer and more distilled. The clearer and more detailed the vision, the greater the odds are of the physical manifestation of that exact vision appearing in material form. Wavering is not conducive to this powerfully creative process. **Steady focus is key**.

The next phase of the creation process is to mobilize our vision - to give applicable life to it. It is our **feelings** about a thing that determine our **belief** in, and conviction about a thing. When we feel passion about a particular vision, our belief and conviction grows stronger, ultimately enabling us to produce it. Conversely, when our emotional confidence and belief in the vision wavers, the likelihood of creating what we envisioned, consequently disintegrates. Human beings bring about the mobilization of vision through the integration of imagery into our E-motions (Energy in Motion). From this emotional immersion and bathing process, a crystal clear visualization is painted, finally making its way onto the canvas of our lives in the material world, in a physical form that we can now experience through the bodily senses.

Now we have a clear vision – an active mental blueprint from which to build and mold more of what we want. Without vision, an idea will perish. People, and entire nations perish without it. Any vision for living together harmoniously is currently marred by war and conflict. We have forgotten - that what makes us all so different – is, in fact, what also makes us so great. Visualize, Feel, Believe that we can do better. Because We Can.

"*Your life is an occasion. Rise To It!*" – Suzanne Weyn

28 CC   RISE

How do you view your life? Do you view it as some mundane, fixed existence, filled with tribulation and circumstance? Do you imagine life as an event over which you have little to no control? Do you shy away from what you think might be awaiting you out there; or do you anxiously welcome whatever it is – eager to crash into it like a stunt person readies for their next great feat? I encourage you to embrace the 'take life by the horns' approach to living. Novelist Suzanne Weyn proposes that life is an occasion, and that we should – as with any other occasion – rise to! I like this philosophy, and I hope you do, too!

So, what is an **occasion**? In this context, we are referring to **a special or important time, event, ceremony, or juncture**. We do tend to 'rise' to many of life's events or occasions, but we don't necessarily rise to the occasion of life *itself*. When a child is born, we rise to the occasion in celebration to welcome his arrival, supporting the new mother and father in every way. When a couple announces their decision to wed, family and friends rise to the occasion in support of their union. We don't tend to view life outside of these special occasions, as a special occasion. These special proceedings are in many cases a once-in-a-lifetime occurrence, whereas life is happening every single moment. It is imperative that we rise to the occasion of our life – for it is the most important occasion of all!

Life is awaiting you! I challenge you to rise to the occasion of it, approaching each day as the miraculous occasions they are. Billions of critical bodily functions must operate in perfect unison and order, as to enable you to rise from your slumber each morning. Never take life for granted; anchor within your heart a determination to see every single day as a chance to be born anew – an opportunity to re-set the clock and start over, creating a continuous occasion of your life that you can be most proud of. Rise up now! And Godspeed.

*"Life is a song – sing it.
Life is a game – play it.
Life is a challenge – meet it.
Life is a dream – realize it.
Life is a sacrifice – offer it.
Life is love – enjoy it."* - Sai Baba

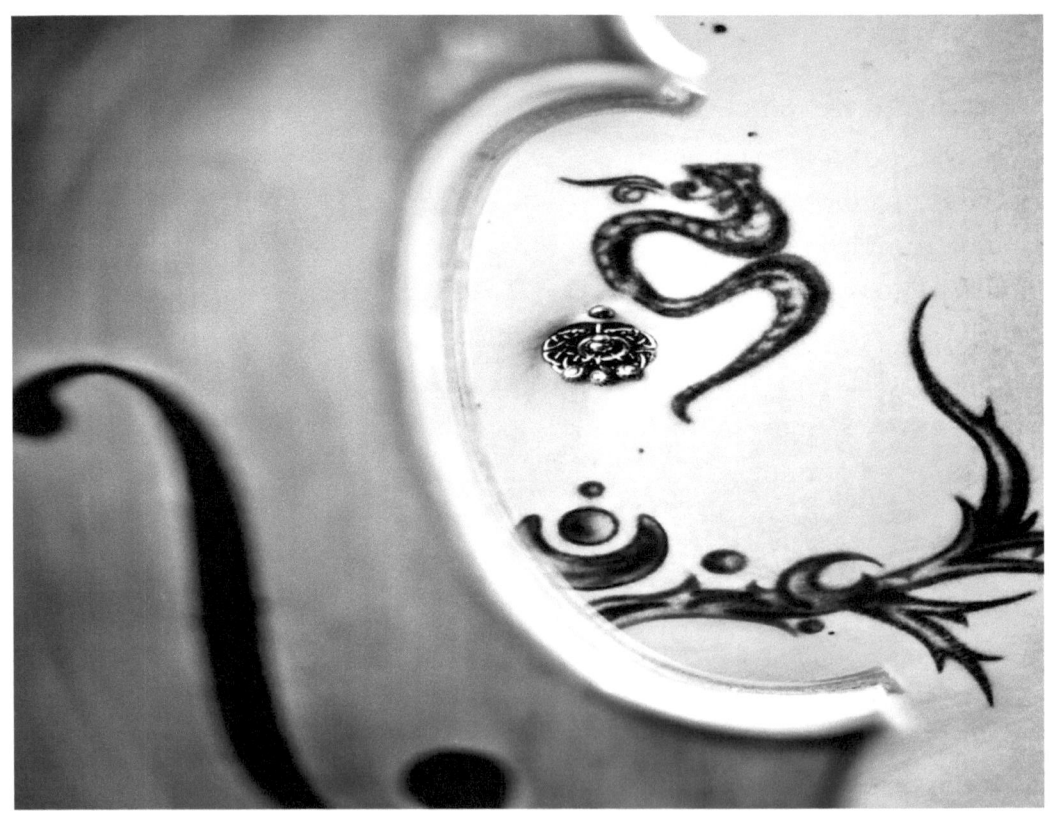

29 CC   LIFE IS A GAME – PLAY IT WELL

The dream of Life is a Game – one in which we are all participants, either consciously or unconsciously. The roles we are free to choose are endless and interchangeable at any time. Some choose the role of a doctor; others choose to become lawyers, scientists, entertainers, thieves, caregivers, clergymen, and more. Do you like to play games? Apparently so, because you came here to play. So you may as well put forth your best effort.

No matter your chosen role in the moment, The Game of life is chock full of obstacles for you to overcome and grow; spoils are waiting to be won in your victories. With the right mental disposition, you could easily crush it at every level. It's like learning to become the most graceful dancer. Learning to dance with life gracefully is the ultimate evidence of how well you play The Game. Close your eyes. See yourself spinning and twirling in perfect harmony with Everything That Is. In your dreams there are no restrictions, are there? In your dreams you are able to perform extraordinary feats, can't you? In that space, you can tune directly into whatever is lurking in the corners of your subconscious mind, and summon it to stand at attention. You can perform whatever magical art form through which you choose to express the spirit of your essence. For in these roles, it is your Soul's desire to express!

What wonderful good we do for the world when we offer up our life as a sacrifice, by parading around proudly, performing our own unique dance. By this act alone, we encourage others to also express freely. It is not, however, about whose performance is best; it is not about competition at all. It is about realizing that every song, dance, or act, though aesthetically different, is majestic. It is about grasping the importance of everything living life out loud and on purpose - creating the uniqueness that can only subsist by the permutation of it ALL.

"Love makes your soul crawl out from its hiding place." – Zora Neal Hurston

30 CC   NO MORE HIDING

Love: perhaps one of the most controversial, complex, and elusive concepts in human history. It is a 'concept' because it is an abstract idea that humanity has had a very difficult time understanding. A handful have passed through, making exceptional attempts at enlightening us on what this powerful force called **Love** really is. People do all sorts of things in the name of **Love** – some actions appear to be sane, while others indubitably irrational. The effects that so-called Love can have on an individual will fluctuate based on their varying interpretations of it.

Love, according to my own interpretation, seems to be in alignment with the late Nora Hurston's – "**Love** makes your soul crawl out from its hiding place". You see, when we choose to walk in complete **Love**, feelings of guilt and confusion melt away; an epic cleansing takes place. Feelings of inadequacy, regret, and self-doubt fade into the background when **Love** is present. Acceptance – of you, of others, and of whatever life brings your way – quickly takes the place of any fear. Slowly, and without bound, the root of who you are begins to surface. From a dry and rigid foundation, they begin to sprawl out to connect with the nurturing moisture **Love** gives. **Love** is shameless; it causes our Soul to creep out from among the shadows. It spreads the full breadth of its wings like a bald eagle in preparation to ascend toward the heavens. It swoops down to share the wind of its mighty span. When you awaken to the fact that **Love** is truly all there is, your Soul will no longer seek camouflage. For **Love** has no fear, and without fear's presence, the Soul's sole intention shines brighter, sharing the treasure it has found of itself. Compassion and empathy flow like a spring gushing limitlessly, radiating from deep within the heart's epicenter.

Beloved, this is your true Soul; this is who you really are. Hide no more – no one is judging you. No one *can* judge you. Be true. Keep reaching up toward the light of the **Love** that you are. It is time for You to come out now.

"When you think everything is someone else's fault, you will suffer a lot." – Dalai Lama

31 CC   THE BLAME GAME

The blame game – we all play it. I suppose it is safe to say that we have all, at one time or another, projected blame onto someone else. This usually occurs as a result of some suffering we have undergone. When we blame others for our own anguish – instead of considering that perhaps it is something we attracted to ourselves for reasons yet to be discovered – we only volley the negativity back and forth to each other. We never allow it to have a proper death and burial, and for peace to take its rightful place in our lives. I find there to be no such thing as fault; there is only experience. A computer or its programming can fault; an automobile or airplane can fault; a machine inside of a factory can fault. Human beings can only experience - by which so-called suffering might occur as a result. Blaming others for this perceived suffering only aggravates it; blaming others prolongs the course of healing.

No matter how badly you may want to, you cannot control what others do. You cannot control whether or not they apologize, or exhibit any empathy or compassion for any pain or suffering you believe they have caused you. You can, however, take full responsibility for how you respond – this is how inner peace is obtained. When someone fails to handle a situation in the way you think he/she should have, and you suffer as a result of this perceived mishandling, the blame game often begins; followed by more self-inflicted suffering. When we make the brave decision to look only at ourselves, we quarantine suffering, and thereby invite more peace and emotional balance into our lives.

Stop the blame game; own your experience. Consciously and thoughtfully choose your responses. You are hereby granted the power to do so – as if you really needed my permission.

"Wherever you are is just fine...you can get to wherever you want to be from wherever you are. It's time to stop measuring where you are in relation to where anybody else is. The only factor that has anything to do with you is where you are in relationship to where you want to be." - Abraham

32 CC — THIS IS THE WAY

Wherever you are in your life, you are in many ways there because you have chosen to be. Where you are is largely a result of decisions you have made up until this point, with few exceptions. Some made incarnate, others pre-incarnate. Even if you believe that some decisions were made for you, today, you can decide to switch directions. If you desire to be in a different place in life - and haven't been able to make that shift - it is only because you have not made the uncompromising decision and agreement with yourself to do so. Making a firm declaration at the heart level is where the surfacing of a new reality commences.

Here's the good news: *If you are unhappy with where you are today and wish to change it, you are only <u>decisions</u> away from where you want to be. Today is your day!*

What if you are not able to make an 'about-face' today? So what! There is tomorrow. Then there is tomorrow again. And what about tomorrow? This is not a license to procrastinate, but a nudging to acknowledge and show gratitude for the process involved in manifesting change in your life. What impedes your progression from where you are to where you want to be, is your tendency to compare your journey to the journeys of others. Their path is not yours; their challenges are not yours; their circumstances are not yours. So what good does it do you to measure by a comparison of apples to oranges? None.

This Is The Way: 1) **Decide**; 2) **Eliminate the comparisons**; 3) **Appreciate where you are and your own unique path**; and 4) **Consider only where *you* are in relationship to where *you* want to be**.

No particular starting point leads to where you want to be; you can get there from ANYWHERE, especially in a world filled with infinite avenues by which to travel. Pick one, and get moving!

"It's not what you look at that matters; it's what you see." - Henry David Thoreau

33 CC   YOUR VIEWING APPARATUS

We have all heard the sayings, *is the glass half empty or is it half full?* Or...*beauty is in the eye of the beholder*. The presumption of these adages is that it is the observer who determines what it is they see, not the object. The glass is neither half empty nor half full, until the observer decides which of these is so.

What we see and what we are looking at can be drastically different. **The optimist may say**: the glass is half full or 'those flowers are gorgeous'; whereas **the pessimist may say**: the glass is half empty or 'those flowers are repulsive'. Both are correct. What they have determined to be truth - about the flowers or about the glass - is based solely upon how each of them has chosen to see it; it is not determined by the object they are actually looking at.

Take abstract art: two people can look at the exact same piece and interpret something entirely different. Perception works this way – multiple people observing the same thing, yet seeing something different. Allow your mind to focus only upon what it is you *want* to see versus what it is you are looking at. Your imagination is a powerfully creative tool! In it resides an endless reservoir of ideas, possibilities, and combinations to get it done. A silver lining resides within every single 'cloud' in life - you only have to concentrate on seeing the lining as opposed to the cloud that is obscuring your view. Focusing on the lining causes the cloud to fade slowly into the background, allowing the bright and silvery lining to emerge as the dominant image.

We are all observing life with the camera of our mind – with different lenses and filters affixed, crafted after our individual experiences. These lenses are highly flexible; they can be removed, adjusted, cleaned, or replaced at any time. So if you don't like what you are seeing in your life, more than likely it has something to do with your viewing apparatus. **Change it**.

"Gratitude is a fullness of heart that moves you from limitation and fear to expansion and love." – Deepak Chopra

34 CC   THE GREATNESS OF GRATITUDE

One of the greatest gifts you can give back to your life is gratitude – gratitude for all that life gives to you. Why does life need you to give back to it? Well - it doesn't, actually. Life *needs* nothing from you, but giving life gratitude produces for you a plethora of nourishments to feast from; it produces a smorgasbord from which you can indulge and share. Gratitude is the doorway to abundance. It is also the gateway to forgiveness. The more grateful you become, the portals of abundance and forgiveness literally pop off the hinges, bulging forth with excess. Your cup fills, and spills over with the astonishing stuff of life!

Want more succulence out of life? Be grateful for what you already have. It can be difficult at times to notice the abundance surrounding you; sometimes you can't seem to find clarity through all the muck in your path. Life's unexpectedness can cause you to look down instead of looking upward, where your perspectives of gratitude are much more easily broadened and realized. So always look up! Want more love – then spread love. Let love flood every canal of your life, while showing gratitude for the love that is in front of you. Want more wealth – be a good steward over the wealth you already have, no matter how big or small. Want better health – be grateful for the health you now enjoy. Want more happiness – be happy, and be grateful for the happiness that others share with you. Want more of anything – be grateful for everything. Your heart will fill exponentially.

There are so many things to be grateful for. Walk outside, take a stroll. There is wonderment and miracles in every stride. The cool breeze that dries your perspiring flesh. The sun's rays beaming down, bountifully providing light and life to all underneath its care. Children in the park, laughing jovially - swinging the swings, riding the stationary caterpillar as if it were alive. And it is. The young have not a care in the world - talk about living in the moment! Can we return to the solace and peace of mind of a child? Yes! A resounding - Yes!

"The answer is never the answer. What's really interesting is the mystery. If you seek the mystery instead of the answer, you'll always be seeking. I've never seen anyone really find the answer – they think they have so they stop thinking and seeking. But the job is to seek the mystery, to evoke mystery."- Unknown

35 CC   SEEK THE MYSTERY

Mysterious is the word that best describes existence; it is also the backbone of all what we believe existence to be. We are born, we live, then we die; without a clue as to what happens next. Many die without ever having truly lived. I refuse to not live this life fully! I want to experience the mystery of life in all of its grandeur!

Though many claim to, no one actually knows the answer to any of it; and that's the actual beauty of it – the mystery. It is all an enormous web of total ambiguity, laced with such intricate detail that literally baffles the mind. Any reasoning or logic that anyone can provide - no matter how brilliant it may sound - is only a presupposition; pure speculation and theory, based entirely around stories and myths passed down through cultural, tribal, religious and social circles over an untold number of generations. Speculation and theory can lead to deep and uncompromising beliefs and personal truths, but there is not a singular answer that can possibly serve us all. Perhaps Love could. But even love is a personal truth.

So chase the mystery instead - chasing the anonymity evokes more and greater mystique. This is where life really comes alive! Pursuit of the mystery is far more fun than chasing an ever-elusive 'answer'. It's like reading a good mystery novel series, that when one book ends, a hatch is left open for an adjoining story to commence. This creates new places for the mind to explore, and in life, they are endless.

We find only stress and displeasure when we expect to find an answer that simply cannot be found, because it does not exist. Whatever 'answers' we do find, only lead us to another piece of the mystery. Spend your life chasing the mystery, not the answer; you will find life to be a lot more interesting, meaningful, invigorating, and ignitable!

Open up your eyes, and see-k!

"It is not the mountain we conquer, but ourselves." - Edmund Hillary

36 CC   CONQUERING THE MOUNTAIN THAT IS YOU

The journey of life is akin to climbing a mountain layered with elevated flats and steeped with inclines. You can only come to truly appreciate - and ultimately enjoy the flats - after you have faced and conquered the inclines. I have conquered many inclines in my life, and to a great degree of personal satisfaction. You will learn as I have that with every conquest and conquering of one mountain, grows within you a newfound confidence that the next one is also conquerable.

In what I once perceived as mistakes or failures in life, I discovered were mere miscalculations yielding lessons learned. By continually applying these learned lessons, it becomes easier and more gratifying to stand atop the next mountain victorious.

> **Every part of your journey is a victory; another step towards the mastery of YOU.**

The mountain of the Self is higher and more challenging than Mt. Everest, but with each incremental climb upward, you will master a deeper level of YOU. Marvelous discoveries await you, should you choose to consciously explore the uncharted depths of your Soul. Every landing allows for a moment to exhale - to rest and reflect on the journey in its wholeness. Constant cogitation lends the opportunity to finally accept and concede that there really is no end. The valleys of desperation are just as beautiful as the peaks that impart a bird's eye view that enables you to bask in the mountain's gentle breeze as you look out over the embers and ashes from which an improved version of YOU victoriously arose.

Peaks and valleys are one in the same, and once you truly know YOU in your divinity, you can see your Self clearly in any juxtaposition. Conquering YOU - that is the most coveted prize of life.

"If you love a flower, don't pick it up - because if you pick it up it dies, and it ceases to be what you love. So if you love a flower let it be. Love is not about possession. Love is about appreciation."- Osho

37 CC — LEAVE THE FLOWER BE

As humans living in the modern world, we have a great tendency to want to possess things we find to be beautiful; we like to own things so that we can behold its beauty at will. We may do this with a beautiful flower, or a bouquet of flowers; we may do the same with some other unique piece taken from nature, perhaps out of aspirations to display it in another place to share its beauty with others in a different space and time. What we often fail to realize in doing this, is that once removed it is no longer the thing we originally fell in love with. We have altered it in ways we don't often realize. We have taken from it the very elements that made it beautiful to begin with. Its natural tendencies, the love that poured into its laborious development, the support systems that helped form the beauty we adored so much – we have now distorted.

Take the case of the picked flower - Sure, it may look, feel, even smell like the flower you initially encountered before picking it - but it isn't. Once the flower is plucked from its natural habitat, forced to become something it is not, nothing about it is ever the same. It has become something all together different, as its comfortable and familiar surroundings have been stripped away; which were the constituents so conducive in producing the beauty you appreciated in it so much. In this plucking, we sacrifice a lifetime of beauty for momentary pleasure.

Now think of your relationships - Love the people in your life just as they are. Release the need to change them, and allow them to grow from where they are. Nourish them where they stand. Do not pluck them just so you can own and control them; or you will - perhaps unknowingly, but inexcusably - begin the dying process of the very thing you once loved so much. **Let them be**.

"Everything must die in order to live!"
- Bradford Speaks

38 CC   THE BEAUTY OF DYING

The beauty of new life that many parts of our world experiences during Spring, would not be possible if Winter had not occurred just prior. Without Winter, Spring could not exist. Think of the onset of Winter, and how the plants, flowers, and trees all retreat, attempting to sidestep the bitter temperatures and cold winds that characterize the Winter season. In many areas, birds will fly toward the direction of warmer climates. This brief hiatus (or death) from their usual environment enables them to live in it again at a future date, when conditions are better suited for their long-term survival. All things living must experience death - a brief departure or separation from life - in order to live again.

The story of the god-man, Jesus - who realized the value of his life by finding true and divine alignment with The Infinite Source within him - is the most widely known and popularized of the god-man stories today. The story – figuratively, but clearly – illustrates how man must die to his self so that he may reconnect with his Self at a future point in time; this he must do in order to experience enlightenment, or an awakening to his Divine Self while in the body. Esoterically speaking, the story was less about a literal crucifixion and resurrection, and more about awakening to the fact that we should welcome 'death', as it must occur in order for life to begin again - in a new form, with a brand new configuration of mind and Spirit. Without this figurative death that these stories speak to, the spiritual transformation they all experienced would not have been possible. Death is what precedes life.

Isn't it enlightening to finally inner-stand that there is just as much beauty in dying as there is in living? It is the dying to self that makes living so much richer. If we want to live our lives at the highest levels possible, we must all die to the one-sided re-presentation of ourselves that has been so eloquently articulated to us by the ego.

~ Be willing to die, so that you may finally live ~

"Our deepest fear is not that we are inadequate. Our deepest fear is that we are powerful beyond measure." – Maryanne Williamson

39 CC   YOU ARE POWERFUL

Even in light of many remarkable human advancements in the areas of Math, Science, Technology, and the Arts, the height of human potentiality is still vastly unknown. Achievements beyond what we have already manifested, are corralled only by what we can believe, and are ironically catapulted by the same. When you finally arrive to the point of shifting your beliefs about yourself and about your potential, from a position of limitation to one of limitless-ness, your potential for greatness will be unleashed. Most of us never reach this level of belief about ourselves. Why does it seem that - in the famous words of rapper Drake – "everybody dies, but not everybody lives"? Such truths often ooze out to us from pop culture, as life continues along its journey of imitating art. You are free to break free of these shackles when you're ready. Together we have the power to create worlds. This wonderful gift of life we have been given is eveidence of such, and is perhaps even a duty we all share. What we believe about ourselves can serve to greatly restrict us, or expand us.

Broaden your perspectives, and an entirely new world will begin to unfold. Insist on seeing that life - in all of its circumstance – is always wonderful and dripping with the nectar of experience. Placing such a demand on always seeing the best in everything, will create within you a healthy anxiety and excitement that thrusts you out of bed each day.

Play more - stop taking life so seriously, and allow more fun to meander in. This is not a suggestion, but a directive. Peace and happiness are always available to you. Even in the midst of life's most chaotic and disheartening moments, you are surrounded by love. Look at you…see how powerful you are! Relinquish fear. Go forward; live boldly in the power of the love that you are. Inadequate? Psssh! You are more than enough - you always have been!

"If you are one whom within your relationships must always win, know that you never will."
– Bradford Speaks

40 CC   BEING RIGHT IS OUR GREATEST WRONG

Relationships are one of the most predominant aspects of the human experience. Everything is in constant relationship with everything else - be it consciously or unconsciously. These relationships are not limited between persons and other persons. As human beings, we are in relationship with the fabrics that weave together the garments we wear; the foods that we consume to preserve life and health; the moon and sun that fill our day and night skies with light; right down to the very air we breathe. It is all a part of US!

Romantic relationships with other human beings are where many of us expend a large portion of our energy. These relationships seem to consume our lives the most, and though their tumultuousness is a necessary dynamic for spawning enriching experiences and spiritual prosperity, all too often we cause ourselves much more pain than is necessary.

In my experience with coaching couples, one thing I have found to be a common thread is this need to be 'right'. Can't we all just agree upfront that either no one is right, or better yet, both are? Either way is fine, and this agreement diffuses all the drama beforehand. We are simply coming from different perspectives, shaped by our variations of internal and external experience. Our mishandling of this particular dynamic brings about a combative element that can erect a win/lose philosophy – a philosophy in which no one ever really wins.

At some level, being 'right' fulfills something inside of us. But is the damage this need foments really worth it? No. The exoneration of yourself from this destructive need is immensely liberating. Try it. For a day, let it be acceptable for you to be wrong in the eyes of your partner, sibling, co-worker, parent, or friend. Teach them through *your* example in humility. You are always in control because you always have a choice. Eradicate the need to be right, and begin to *right* the ship of your relationships.

"Darkness cannot drive out darkness; only light can do that. Hate cannot drive out hate; only love can do that."
– Dr. Martin Luther King, Jr.

2 X DOSE   ONLY LIGHT CAN DRIVE OUT DARKNESS

I wasn't yet alive to witness his rise to prominence, his massive intercontinental presence, and the movement of millions that his energy was able to awaken and mobilize. But one of the most remarkable qualities I have been able to glean from what I have studied and understood about the life of esteemed negro American Civil Rights icon and martyr, Martin Luther King, Jr., has been his profound level of awareness of the power of love, and its relationship to attaining peace and change in the world. He knew intuitively that fighting darkness with darkness was futile. As he saw it, the only way to cast out darkness was to flood it with light. Love emits such a light - that when cast upon darkness - can only leave a remnant shadow containing a small window where darkness once stood.

An argument can certainly be made about how *darkness* is defined. For the sake of this Injection, we will define darkness as: any actions that do not feel good to the human Soul; anything that repels against the intrinsic good present in man. Darkness is the antithesis of light. Further, darkness equates to fear and hate; light, on the other hand, equates to Love and Kindness. Light and darkness cannot co-exist within the same space, and the awareness of one cannot exist without the awareness of its opposite. In other words, we cannot recognize light until know what darkness looks like. If we want our lives to feel good - or be filled with more light (love) and absent of darkness (fear) - we only need to allow the light of love to shine through us.

We have this choice to make daily – to either project our life as a force of darkness or as a force of light. If we want to drive out darkness from our lives, the answer is pretty obvious - set your intention to always emanate light. We must project a collective and undeniable luminosity out onto the world stage. We must infect others with our Light.

Stand up - and let us all shine bright together.

MIS AMORES

ABOUT THE AUTHOR

Bradford Speaks is a Life Architect, Relationship Coach, Speaker and Author. He specializes in individual life transformations in the areas of Life Performance, Relationship Enhancement, and Yoga & Spirituality.

After the derailment of his second marriage in twenty years, Bradford Speaks embarked upon a Hero's Journey of sorts - an extraordinary expedition of self-discovery! Meeting both villains and guides along his path, his intent was to discover the answers to sustaining a deep, happy and fulfilling existence, regardless of what obstacles life might bring one's way.

40 CCs of Inspiration embodies many of his personal discoveries; its words illustrate in many ways how his experience with love and the myth of heartbreak, shattered his model of the world, forcing him to piece it back together in a more fluid form than ever before. Doing so allowed him to discover who he really is. Within these pages, Coach Speaks shares his own experiences, in hopes of not only delighting readers, but inspiring, encouraging, enlightening, and motivating them to blaze their own pathway toward infinite joy.

Coach Speaks resides in sunny Southern California, and is the father of six amazing human beings (4 young ladies and 2 young men) – Bradford II, Jahna, Christyn, Blaise, Jackson, and Claire. He recently welcomed his first grandchild into the world - hello, Blaire Elizabeth!